ISBN 978-1-332-88605-0
PIBN 10432576

This book is a reproduction of an important historical work. Forgotten Books uses state-of-the-art technology to digitally reconstruct the work, preserving the original format whilst repairing imperfections present in the aged copy. In rare cases, an imperfection in the original, such as a blemish or missing page, may be replicated in our edition. We do, however, repair the vast majority of imperfections successfully; any imperfections that remain are intentionally left to preserve the state of such historical works.

1 MONTH OF
FREE
READING

at
www.ForgottenBooks.com

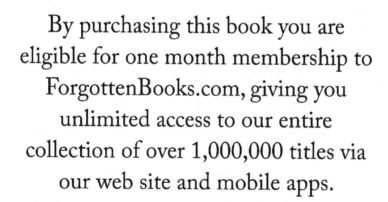

By purchasing this book you are eligible for one month membership to ForgottenBooks.com, giving you unlimited access to our entire collection of over 1,000,000 titles via our web site and mobile apps.

To claim your free month visit:
www.forgottenbooks.com/free432576

English
Français
Deutsche
Italiano
Español
Português

www.forgottenbooks.com

Mythology Photography **Fiction**
Fishing Christianity **Art** Cooking
Essays Buddhism Freemasonry
Medicine **Biology** Music **Ancient**
Egypt Evolution Carpentry Physics
Dance Geology **Mathematics** Fitness
Shakespeare **Folklore** Yoga Marketing
Confidence Immortality Biographies
Poetry **Psychology** Witchcraft
Electronics Chemistry History **Law**
Accounting **Philosophy** Anthropology
Alchemy Drama Quantum Mechanics
Atheism Sexual Health **Ancient History**
Entrepreneurship Languages Sport
Paleontology Needlework Islam
Metaphysics Investment Archaeology
Parenting Statistics Criminology
Motivational

UPON

SLAVERY.

THE FIFTH EDITION.

By JOHN WESLEY, A. M.

LONDON:

Printed by G. PARAMORE, North Green, Worship-Street;
and sold by G. *Whitfield*, at the Chapel, City-Road; and at the
Methodist Preaching-Houses, in Town and Country. 1792.

[Price TWO-PENCE]

T H O U G H T S

U P O N

S L A V E R Y.

1. **B**Y *Slavery* I mean Domeſtic Slavery, or that of a ſervant to a maſter. A late ingenious Writer well obſerves, " The variety of forms in which Slavery appears, makes it almoſt impoſſible to convey a juſt notion of it, by way of definition. There are however certain propeities which have accompanied Slavery in moſt places, whereby it is eaſily diſtinguiſned from that mild domeſtic *fervice* which obtains in our country." *

2. *Slavery* imports an obligation of perpetual ſervice, an obligation which only the conſent of the maſter can diſſolve. Neither in ſome countries can the maſter himſelf diſſolve it, without the conſent of judges appointed by the law. It generally gives the maſter an arbitraiy power of any correction, not affecting life or limb. Sometimes even theſe are expoſed to his will : or protected only by a fine, or ſome ſlight puniſhment, too inconſiderable to reſtrain a maſter of a harſh temper. It creates an incapacity of acquiring any thing, except for the maſter's benefit. It allows the maſter to alienate the Slave, in the ſame manner as his cows and horſes. Laſtly it deſcends in its full extent from parent to child, even to the laſt generation.

3. The beginning of this may be dated from the remoteſt period, of which we have an account in hiſtory. It commenced in the barbarous ſtate of Society, and in proceſs of time ſpread into all nations. It prevailed particularly among the *Jews*, the *Greeks*, the *Romans*, and the ancient *Germans :* and was tranſmitted by them to the various kingdoms and ſtates, which aroſe out of the *Roman* empire. But after chriſtianity prevailed, it gradually fell into decline in almoſt all parts of *Europe*. This great change began in *Spain*, about the end of the eighth century : and was become general in moſt other kingdoms of *Europe*, before the middle of the fourteenth.   A 2   4. From

* See Mr. *Hargrave's* Plea for *Somerſet* the Negro.

. 4. From this time Slavery was nearly extinct, till the commencement of the sixteenth century, when the discovery of *America*, and of the Western and Eastern coasts of *Africa*, gave occasion to the revival of it. It took its rise from the *Portuguese*, who to supply the *Spaniards* with men, to cultivate their new possessions in *America*, procured Negroes from *Africa*, whom they sold for Slaves to the *American* Spaniards. This began in the year 1508, when they imported the first Negroes into *Hispaniola*. In 1540, *Charles* the fifth, then King of *Spain*, determined to put an end to *Negro-Slavery :* giving positive orders, That all the Negro-Slaves in the *Spanish* dominions should be set free. And this was accordingly done by *Lagasca*, whom he sent and impowered to free them all, on condition of continuing to labour for their masters. But soon after *Lagascar* returned to *Spain*, Slavery returned and flourished as before. Afterwards other nations, as they acquired possessions in *America*, followed the examples of the *Spaniards ;* and Slavery has taken deep root in most of our *American* colonies.

II. Such is the nature of Slavery : such the beginning of Negro-Slavery in *America*. But some may desire to know, what country it is, from which the Negroes are brought ? What sort of men, of what temper and behaviour are they in their own country ? And in what manner they are generally procured, carried to, and treated in *America* ?

· 1. And first, What kind of country is that from whence they are brought ? Is it so remarkably horrid, dreary and barren, that it is a kindness to deliver them out of it ? I believe many have apprehended so : but it is an entire mistake, if we may give credit to those who have lived many years therein, and could have no motive to misrepresent it.

· 2. That part of *Africa* whence the Negroes are brought, commonly known by the name of *Guinea*, extends along the coast, in the whole, between three and four thousand miles. From the river *Senegal*, (seventeen degrees North of the line) to Cape *Sierra Leona*, it contains seven hundred miles. Thence it runs Eastward about fifteen hundred miles, including the *Grain-coast*, the *Ivory-coast*, the *Gold-coast*, and the *Slave-coast*, with the large kingdom of *Benin*. From thence

thence it runs Southward, about twelve hundred miles; and contains the kingdoms of *Congo* and *Angola.*

3. Concerning the firft, the *Senegal* coaft, Monf. *Bene,* who lived there fixteen years, after defcribing its fruitfulnefs near the fea, fays, "The farther you go from the fea, the more fruitful and well-improved is the country, abounding in pulfe, Indian corn, and various fruits. Here are vaft meadows, which feed large herds of great and fmall cattle. And the villages which lie thick, fhew the country is well peopled." And again: "I was furprized, to fee the land fo well cultivated; fcarce a fpot lay unimproved: the low lands divided by fmall canals, were all fowed with rice: the higher grounds were planted with Indian corn, and peas of different forts. Their beef is ex-cellent; poultry plenty, and very cheap, as are all the neceffaries of life."

4. As to the *Grain* and *Ivory-coaft,* we learn from eye-witneffes, that the foil is in general fertile, producing abundance of rice and roots. Indigo and cotton thrive without cultivation. Fifh is in great plenty; the flocks and herds are numerous, and the trees loaden with fruit.

5. The *Gold-coaft* and *Slave-coaft,* all who have feen it agree; is exceeding fruitful and pleafant, producing vaft quantities of rice and other grain, plenty of fruit and roots, palm-wine and oil, and fifh in great abun-dance, with much tame and wild cattle. The very fame account is given us of the foil and produce of the king-doms of *Benin, Congo* and *Angola.* From which it ap-pears, that *Guinea* in general, is far from a horrid, dreary, barren country, is one of the moft fruitful, as well as the moft pleafant countries in the known world. It is faid indeed to be unhealthy. And fo it is to ftrangers, but perfectly healthy to the native in-habitants.

6. Such is the country from which the Negroes are brought. We come next to enquire, What fort of men they are, of what temper and behaviour, not in our plantations, but in their native country. And here likewife the fureft way is to take our account from eye and ear-witneffes. Now thofe who have lived in the *Senegal* country obferve, it is inhabited by three nations, the *Jalofs, Fulis* and *Mandingos.* The king of the *Jalofs*

has

has under him feveral Minifters, who affift in the exercife of juftice, the Chief Juftice goes in circuit through all his dominions, to hear complaints and determine controverfies. And the Viceroy goes with him, to infpect the behaviour of the *Alkadi,* or Governor of each village. The *Fulis* are governed by their chief men, who rule with much moderation. Few of them will drink any thing ftronger than water, being ftrict *Mahometans.* The government is eafy, becaufe the people are of a quiet and good difpofition ; and fo well inftructed in what is right, that a man who wrongs another is the abomination of all.—They defire no more land than they ufe, which they cultivate with great care and induftry : if any of them are known to be made Slaves by the white men ; they all join to redeem them. They not only fupport all that are old, or blind, or lame among themfelves ; but have frequently fupplied the neceffities of the *Mandingos,* when they were diftreft by famine.

7. The *Mandingos,* fays Monf. *Brue,* are right *Mahometans,* drinking neither wine nor brandy. They are induftrious and laborious, keeping their ground well cultivated, and breeding a good ftock of cattle. Every town has a Governor, and he appoints the labour of the people. The men work the ground defigned for corn ; the women and girls, the rice-ground. He afterwards divides the corn and rice, among them : and decides all quarrels, if any arife. All the Mahometan Negroes conftantly go to public prayers thrice a day : there being a Prieft in every village, who regularly calls them together : and it is furprifing to fee the modefty, attention and reverence which they obferve during their worfhip—Thefe three nations practife feveral trades ; they have Smiths, Sadlers, Potters and Weavers. And they are very ingenious at their feveral occupations. Their Smiths not only make all the inftruments of iron, which they have occafion to ufe, but likewife work many things neatly in gold and filver. It is chiefly the women and children who weave fine cotton cloth, which they dye blue and black.

8. It was of thefe parts of *Guinea,* that Monf. *Adanfon,* Correfpondent of the Royal Academy of Sciences at *Paris,* from 1749, to 1753, gives the following account, both as to the country and people, "Which way foever
I turned

I turned my eyes, I beheld a perfect image of pure na-.
ture : an agreeable folitude, bounded on every fide by
a charming landſcape ; the rural fituation of cottages,
in the midſt of trees ; the eaſe and quietnefs of the
Negroes, reclined under the fhade of the fpreading
foliage, with the fimplicity of their drefs and manners :
the whole revived in my mind the idea of our firſt
parents, and I feemed to contemplate the world in its
primitive ſtate. They are, generally fpeaking, very
good natured, fociable and obliging. I was not a little
pleafed with my firſt reception, and it fully convinced
me, that there ought to be a confiderable abatement,
made, in the accounts we have of the favage character
of the *Africans*." He adds, " It is amazing that an il-
literate people fhould reafon fo pertinently concerning
the heavenly bodies. There is no doubt, but that with
proper inftruments, they would become excellent
aftronomers."

9. The inhabitants of the *Grain* and *Ivory-coaſt* are
reprefented by thole that deal with them, as fenfible,
courteous, and the faireft traders on the coafts of *Guinea*.
They rarely drink to excefs : if any do they are feverely
punifhed by the King's order. They are feldom
troubled with war : if a difference happen between two
nations, they commonly end the difpute amicably.

10. The inhabitants of the *Gold* and *Slave-coaſt* likewife, when they are not artfully incenfed againft each
other, live in great union and friendfhip, being generally well tempered, civil, tractable, and ready to help
any that need it. In particular, the natives of the
kingdom of *Whidah*, are civil, kind, and obliging to
ftrangers. And they are the moft gentleman-like of all
the Negroes, abounding in good manners toward
each other. The inferiors pay the utmoft refpect to
their fuperiors : fo wives to their hufbands, children
to their parents. And they are remarkably induftrious ;
all are conftantly employed ; the men in agriculture,
the women in fpinning and weaving cotton.

11. The *Gold* and *Slave-coaſts* are divided into feveral
diftricts, lome governed by Kings, others by the prin-
cipal men, who take care each of their own town or
village, and prevent or appeafe tumults. They punifh
murder and adultery feverely ; very frequently with
death. Theft and robbery are punifhed by a fine pro-
portionable.

pörtiohable to the goods that were taken.—All the natives. of this coaft, though heathens, believe there is
one God, the Author of them and all things. They
appear likewife to have a confufed apprehenfion of a
future ftate. And accoidingly every town and village
has a place of public woifhip.—It is remarkable that
they have no beggars among them ; fuch is the care of
the chief men, in every city and village, to provide
fome eafy labour, even for the old and weak. Some
are employed in blowing the Smith's bellows ; others
in prefling palm-oil ; others in grinding of colours. If
they are too weak even for this, they fell provifions in
the maiket.

12. The natives of the kingdom of *Benin* are a reafonable and good-natuied people. They are fincere and
inoffenfive, and do no injuftice either to one another
or to ftrangeis. They are eminently civil and courteous :
if you make them a prefent, they endeavour to repay
it double. And if they are trufted, till the fhip returns
the next year, they are fure honeftly to pay the whole
debt. Theft is punifhed among them, although not with
the fame feverity as murder. If a man and woman of
any quality, are taken in adultery, they are certain to
be put to death, and their bodies thrown on a dunghill,
and left a prey to wild beafts. They are punctually
juft and honeft in their dealings ; and are alfo very
charitable : the King and the great Lords taking care to
employ all that are capable of any work. And thofe
that are utterly helplefs they keep for God's fake ; fo
that here alfo are no beggars. The inhabitants of *Congo*
and *Angola* are generally a quiet people. They difcover
a good undeiftanding, and behave in a friendly manner
to ftrangers, being of a mild temper and an affable car-
riage.——Upon the whole therefore the Negroes who
inhabit the coaft of *Africa*, from the river *Senegal* to the
Southern bounds of *Angola*, are fo far from being the
ftupid, fenfelefs, brutifh, lazy barbarians, the fierce,
cruel, perfidious Savages they have been defcribed,
that on the contrary, they are reprefented by them who
have no motive to flatter them, as remarkably fenfible,
confidering the few advantages they have for improving
their underftanding : as induftrious to the higheft degree, perhaps more fo than any other natives of fo warm
a climate : as fair, juft and honeft in all their dealings,
unlefs

unlefs where white men have taught them to be other-wife : and as far more mild, friendly and kind to ftrangers, than any of our forefathers were. Our fore-fathers ! Where fhall we find at this day, among the fair-faced natives of *Europe*, a nation generally prac-tifing the juftice, mercy, and truth, which are found among thefe poor *Africans ?* Suppofe the preceding accounts are true, (which I fee no reafon or pretence to doubt of,) and we may leave *England* and *France*, to feek genuine honefty in *Benin, Congo*, or *Angola*.

III. We have now feen what kind of country it is, from which the Negroes are brought : and what fort of men (even white men being the judges) they were in their own country. Enquire we, thirdly, In what man-ner are they generally procured, carried to, and treated in *America*.

1. *Firft*. In what manner are they procured? Part of them by fraud. Captains of fhips from time to time, invited Negroes to come on board, and then carried them away. But far more have been procured by force. The Chriftians landing upon their coafts, feized as many as they found, men, women and children, and tran-fported them to *America*. It was about 1551, that the *English* began trading to *Guinea :* at firft, for gold and Elephant's teeth, but loon after, for men. In 1556, Sir John Hawkins failed with two fhips to Cape *Verd*, where he fent eighty men on fhore to catch Negroes. But the natives flying, they fell farther down, and there fet the men on fhore, " to burn their towns and take the inhabitants." But they met with fuch re-fiftance, that they had feven men killed, and took but ten Negroes. So they went ftill farther down, till having taken enough, they proceeded to the *Weft-Indies* and fold them.

2. It was fome time before the *Europeans* found a more compendious way of procuring *African* Slaves, by prevailing upon them to make war upon each other, and to fell their prifoners. Till then they feldom had any wars : but were in general quiet and peaceable. But the white men firft taught them drunkennefs and avarice, and then hired them to fell one another. Nay, by this means, even their Kings are induced to fell their own fubjects. So Mr. *Moore* (Factor of the *African* Company in 1730) informs us, " When the King of

Barfalli

Barfalli wants goods or brandy, he fends to the *Englifh* Governor at *James'* Fort, who immediately fends a floop. Againft the time it arrives, he plunders fome of his neighbours' towns, felling the people for the goods he wants. At other times he falls upon one of his own towns, and makes bold to fell his own fubjefts." So Monf. *Brue* fays, "I wrote to the King (not the fame) "if he had a fufficient number of flaves I would treat with him. He feized three hundred of his own people, and fent word, he was ready to deliver them for goods." He adds, "Some of the natives are always ready" (when well pa:d) "to furprize and carry off their own countrymen. They come at night without noife, and if they find any lone cottage, furround it and carry off all the people."—*Barbot*, (another French Faftor) fays, "Many of the Slaves fold by the Negroes are prifoners of war, or taken in the incurfions they make into their enemy's territories. Others are ftolen. Abundance of little Blacks of both fexes, are ftolen away by their neighbours, when found abroad on the road, or in the woods, or elfe in the corn-fields, at the time of year when their parents keep them there all day to fcare away the devouring birds." That their own parents fell them, is utterly falfe : Whites not Blacks, are with-out natural affeftion !

3. To fet the manner wherein Negroes are procured in a yet ftronger light, it will fuffice to give an extraft of two voyages to *Guinea* on this account. The firft is taken verbatim from the original manufcript of the Surgeon's Journal.

"SESTRO, Dec. 29, 1724. No trade to-day, though many traders came on board. They informed us, that the people are gone to war within land, and will bring prifoners enough in two or three days; in hopes of which we ftay.

"The 30th. No trade yet : but our traders came on board to-day, and informed us the people had burnt four towns : fo that to-morrow we expeft flaves off.

"The 31ft, Fair weather; but no trading yet. We fee each night towns burning. But we hear many of the *Seftro* men are killed by the inland Negroes: fo that we fear this war will be unfuccefsful.

"The fecond of January. Laft night we faw a pro-digious fire break out about eleven o'clock, and this

morning

morning fee the town of *Seſtro* burnt down to the
ground." (It contained fome hundred houfes.) " So
that we find their enemies are too hard for them at
prefent, and confequently our trade fpoiled here.
Therefore about feven o'clock we weighed anchor, to
proceed lower down."

4. The fecond Extract taken from the Journal of a
Surgeon, who went from *New-York* on the fame trade,
is as follows. " The Commander of the veffel fent to
acquaint the King, that he wanted a cargo of flaves.
The King promifed to furnifh him, and in order to it,
fet out, defigning to furprize fome town, and make all
the people prifoners. Some time after, the King fent
him word, he had not yet met with the defired fuccefs:
having attempted to break up two towns, but having
been twice repulfed: but that he ftill hoped to procure
the number of Slaves. In this defign he perfifted, till
he met his enemies in the field. A battle was fought,
which lafted three days. And the engagement was fo
bloody, that four thoufand five hundred men were flain
upon the fpot."——Such is the manner wherein the
Negroes are procured! Thus the Chriftians preach the
Gofpel to the Heathens!

5. Thus they are *procured*. But in what numbers and
in what manner are they carried to *America?*——Mr.
Anderſon in his hiftory of Trade and Commerce; ob-
ferves, " *England* fupplies her *American* Colonies with
Negro-flaves, amounting in number to about a hundred
thoufand every year." That is, fo many are taken on
board our fhips; but at leaft ten thoufand of them die
in the voyage: about a fourth part more die at the
different Iflands, in what is called the Seafoning. So
that at an average, in the paffage and feafoning together, thirty thoufand die: that is, properly are murdered. O earth, O fea, cover not thou their blood!

6. When they are brought down to the fhore in order
to be fold, our Surgeons thoroughly examine them, and
that quite naked, women and men, without any dif-
tinction: thofe that are approved are fet on one fide!
In the mean time a burning iron, with the arms or name
of the Company, lies in the fire, with which they are
marked on the breaft. Before they are put into the
fhips, their mafters ftrip them of all they have on their
backs: fo that they come on board ftark naked, women

as well as men. It is common for feveral hundred of them to be put on board one veffel: where they are ftowed together in as little room as it is poffible for them to be crowded. It is eafy to fuppofe what a condition they muft foon be in, between heat, thirft and ftench of various kinds. So that it is no wonder, fo many fhould die in the paffage; but rather that any furvive it.

7. When the veffels arrive at their deftined port, the Negroes are again expofed naked, to the eyes of all that flock together, and the examination of their purchafers; then they are feparated to the plantations of their feveral mafters, to fee each other no more. Here you may fee mothers hanging over their daughters, bedewing their naked breafts with tears, and daughters clinging to their parents, till the whipper foon obliges them to part. And what can be more wretched than the condition they then enter upon? Banifhed from their country, from their friends and relations for ever, from every comfort of life, they are reduced to a ftate fcarce any way preferable to that of beafts of burden. In general a few roots, not of the niceft kind, ufually yams or potatoes, are their food, and two rags, that neither fcreen them from the heat of the day, nor the cold of the night their covering. Their fleep is very fhort, their labour continual, and frequently above their ftrength; fo that death fets many of them at liberty, before they have lived out half their days. The time they work in the *Weft-Indies*, is from day-break to noon, and from two o'clock till dark: during which time they are attended by overfeers, who, if they think them dilatory, or think any thing not fo well done as it fhould be, whip them molt unmercifully, fo that you may fee their bodies long after whealed and fcarred ufually from the fhoulders to the waift. And before they are fuffered to go to their quarters, they have commonly fomething to do, as collecting herbage for the horfes, or gathering fewel for the boilers. So that it is often paft twelve before they can get home. Hence if their food is not prepared, they are fometimes called to labour again, before they can fatisfy their hunger. And no excufe will avail. If they are not in the field immediately, they muft expect to feel the lafh. Did the Creator intend that the nobleft creatures in the vifible world, fhould live fuch a life as this! " Are

" Are *thefe* thy glorious works, Parent of Good ?"

8. As to the punifhment inflicted on them, fays Sir *Hans Sloan*, " they frequently geld them, or chop off half a foot : after they are whipped till they are raw all over. Some put pepper and falt upon them : fome drop melted wax upon their fkin. Others cut off their ears, and conftrain them to broil and eat them. For Rebellion," (that is, afferting their native Liberty, which they have as much right to as to the air they breathe) " they faften them down to the ground with crooked fticks on every limb, and then applying fire by degrees, to the feet and hands, they burn them gradually upward to the head."

9. But will not the laws made in the plantations, prevent or redrefs all cruelty and oppreffion ? We will take but a few of thofe laws for a fpecimen, and then let any man judge.

In order to rivet the chain of flavery, the law of *Virginia* ordains, " That no flave fhall be fet free, upon any pretence whatever, except for fome meritorious fervices, to be adjudged and allowed by the *Governor and Council* : and that where any flave fhall be fet free by his owner, otherwife than is herein directed, the Church-wardens of the parifh wherein fuch negro fhall refide for the fpace of one month are hereby authorized and required, to *take up and fell* the faid negro, by *public outcry*."

Will not thefe Law-givers take effectual care, to prevent cruelty and oppreffion ?

The law of *Jamaica* ordains, " *Every* flave that fhall run away, and continue abfent from his mafter twelve months, fhall be *deemed rebellious* :" And by another law, fifty pounds are allowed, to thofe who kill or bring in alive a *rebellious* flave?" So their law treats thefe poor men with as little ceremony and confideration, as if they were merely brute beafts! But the innocent blood which is fhed in confequence of fuch a deteftable law, muft call for vengeance on the murderous abetters and actors of fuch deliberate wickednefs.

11. But the law of *Barbadoes* exceeds even this, " If any negro under punifhment, by his mafter, or his order, for running away, or any other crime or mif-

demeanor

demeamor, fhall fuffer *in life or member, no perfon whatfoever fhall be liable to any fine therefore.* But if any man, of wantonnefs, or only of bloody-mindednefs or cruel intention, *wilfully kill* a negro of his own" ¡Now obferve the fevere punifhment!) " He fhall pay into the public treafury fifteen pounds fterling! And not be liable to any other punifhment or forfeiture for the fame!"

Nearly allied to this is that law of *Virginia* : " After proclamation is iffued againft llaves that run away, it is lawful for any perfon whatfoever to kill and deftroy fuch flaves, by fuch ways and means as he fhall think fit.

We have feen already fome of the ways and means which have been *thought fit* on fuch occafions. And many more might be mentioned. One Gentleman, when I was abroad, *thought fit* to roaft his flave alive! But if the moft natural act of " running away" from intolerable tyranny, deferves fuch relentlefs feverity, what punifhment have thefe *Law-makers* to expect hereafter, on account of their own enormous offences?

IV. 1. This is the plain, unaggravated matter of fact. Such is the manner wherein our *African* flaves are procured : luch the manner wherein they are removed from their native land, and wherein they are treated in our plantations. I would now enquire, whether thefe things can be defended, on the principles of even heathen honefty? Whether they can be reconciled (fetting the Bible out of the queftion) with any degree of either juftice or mercy?

2. The grand plea is, " They are authorized by law." But can law, Human Law, change the nature of things? Can it turn darknefs into light, or evil into good? By no means. Notwithftanding ten thoufand laws, right is right, and wrong is wrong ftill. There muft ftill remain an effential difference between juftice and injuftice, cruelty and mercy. So that I ftill afk, who can reconcile this treatment of the negroes, firft and laft, with either mercy or juftice?

Where is the juftice of inflicting the fevereft evils, on thofe that have done us no wrong? Of depriving thofe that never injured us in word or deed, of every comfort of life? Of tearing them from their native country,

country, and depriving them of liberty itfelf? To which an *Angolan,* has the fame natural right as an *Englifhman,* and on which he lets as high a value? Yea where is the juftice of taking away the lives of innocent, inoffenfive men? Murdering thoufands of them in their own land, by the hands of their own countrymen: many thoufands, year after year, on fhipboard, and then cafting them like dung into the fea! And tens of thoufands in that cruel flavery, to which they are fo unjuftly reduced?

3. But waving, for the prefent, all other confiderations, I ftrike at the root of this complicated villany. I abfolutely deny all flave-holding to be confiftent with any degree of natural juftice.

I cannot place this in a clearer light, than that great ornament of his profeffion, Judge *Blackftone* has already done. Part of his words are as follows:

"The three origins of the right of flavery affigned by *Juftinian,* are all built upon falfe foundations. 1. Slavery is faid to arife from captivity in war. The conqueror having a right to the life of his captive, if he fpares that, has then a right to deal with them as he fpeaks. But this is untrue, if taken generally, That by the laws of nations, a man has a right to kill his enemy. He has only a right to kill him in particular cafes, in cafes of abfolute neceffity for felf-defence. And it is plain, this abfolute neceffity did not fubfift, fince he did not kill him, but made him prifoner. War itfelf is juftifiable only on principles of felf-prefervation. Therefore it gives us no right over prifoners, but to hinder their hurting us by confining them. Much leis can it give a right to torture, or kill, or even enflave an enemy when the war is over. Since therefore the right of making our prifoners flaves, depends on a fuppofed right of flaughter, that foundation failing, the confequence which is drawn from it muft fail likewife."

" It is faid fecondly, Slavery may begin, by one man's felling himfelf to another. And it is true, a man may fell himfelf to work for another; but he can not fell himfelf to be a flave, as above defined. Every fale implies an equivalent given to the feller, in lieu of what he tranfers to the buyer. But what equivalent can be given for life or liberty? His propeity like-.

wife,

wife, with the very price which he feems to receive,
devolves *ipfo facto* to his mafter, the inftant he becomes
his flave: in this cafe therefore the buyer gives nothing.
Of what validity then can a fale be, which deftroys
the very principle upon which all fales are found-
ed?"

"We are told, Thirdly, that men may be *born flaves*,
by being the children of llaves. But this being built
upon the two former rights muft fall together with
them, if neither captivity, nor contract can by the
plain law of nature and reafon, reduce the parent
to a ftate of flavery, much lefs can they reduce the off-
fpring." It clearly follows, that all flavery is as irre-
concileable to juftice as to mercy.

4. That flave-holding is utterly inconfiftent with
mercy, is almoft too plain to need a proof. Indeed
it is faid, "That thefe negroes being prifoners of war,
our captains and factors buy them, merely to fave them
from being put to death. And is not this mercy?"
I anfwer, 1. Did Sir *John Hawkins*, and many others,
feize upon men, women and children, who were at
peace in their own fields and houfes, merely to fave
them from death? 2. Was it to fave them from death,
that they knock'd out the brains of thofe they could
not bring away? 3. Who occafioned and fomented
thofe wars, wherein thefe poor creatures were taken
prifoners? Who excited them by money, by drink,
by every poffible means, to fall upon one another?
Was it not themfelves? They know in their own confcience it was, if they have any confcience left. But
4. To bring the matter to a fhort iffue. Can they fay
before God, That they ever took a fingle voyage, or
bought a fingle negro from this motive? They cannot, they well know, to get money, not to fave lives,
was the whole and fole fpring of their motions.

5. But if this manner of procuring and tearing negroes is not confiftent either with mercy or juftice, yet
there is a plea for it which every man of bufinefs will
acknowledge to be quite fufficient. Fifty years ago,
one meeting an eminent ftatefman in the lobby of the
Houfe of Commons, faid, "You have been long
talking about juftice and equity, Pray which is this
bill? Equity or juftice?" He anfwered, very fhort,
and plain, "D—n juftice: it is neceffity." Here alfo
the

the flave-holder fixes his foot : here he refts the ftrength·
of his caufe. " If it is not quite right, yet it *muft* be
fo : there is an abfolute *neceffity for it.* It is neceffary
we fhould procure flaves : and when we have procured
them, it is neceffary to ufe them with feverity, confidering their ftupidity, ftubbornnefs and wickednefs."

I anfwer, You ftumble at the threfhold : I deny
that villany is ever neceffary. It is impoffible that it
fhould ever be neceffary, for any reafonable creature
to violate all the laws of juftice, mercy, and truth.
No circumftances can make it neceffary for a man to
burft in funder all the ties of humanity. It can
never be neceffary for a rational being to fink himfelf
below a brute. A man can be under no neceffity, of
degrading himfelf into a wolf. The abfurdity of the
fuppofition is fo glaring, that one would wonder any
one could help feeing it.

6. This in general. But to be more particular, I
afk, 1. What is neceffary ? And fecondly, To what
end ? It may be anfwered, " The whole method now
ufed by the original purchafers of negroes, is neceffary
to the furnifhing our colonies yearly with a hundred
thoufand flaves." I grant this is neceffary to that end.
But how is that end neceffary ? How will you prove
it neceffary that one hundred, that one of thofe flaves
fhould be procured?" " Why, it is neceffary to my
gaining an hundred thoufand pounds." Perhaps fo :
but how is *this* neceffary ? It is very poffible you
might be both a better and a happier man, if you had
not a quarter of it. I deny that your gaining one
thoufand is neceffary, either to your prefent or eternal
happinefs. " But however you muft allow, thefe
flaves are neceffary for the cultivation of our Iflands :
inafmuch as white men are not able to labour in hot
climates." I anfwer, 1. It were better that all thofe
Iflands fhould remain uncultivated for ever, yea, it
were more defirable that they were altogether funk in
the depth of the fea, than that they fhould be cultivated at fo high a price, as the violation of juftice,
mercy and truth. But, fecondly, the fuppofition on
which you ground your argument is falfe. For white
men, even *Englifh* men, are well able to labour in hot
climates : provided they are temperate both in meat

and

and drink, and that they inure themfelves to it by degrees. I fpeak no more than I know by experience.
It appears from the thermometer, that the fummer
heat in *Georgia*, is frequently equal to that in *Barbadoes*, yea to that under the line. And yet I and my
family (eight in number) did employ all our fpare time
there, in felling of trees and clearing of ground, as
hard labour as any negro need be employed in. The
German family likewife, forty in number, were employed in all manner of labour. And this was fo far
from impairing our health, that we all continued perfectly well, while the idle ones round about us, were
fwept away as with a peftilence. It is not true therefore that white men are not able to labour, even in hot
climates, full as well as black. But if they were not,
it would be better that none fhould labour there,
that the work fhould be left undone, than that
myriads of innocent men fhould be murdeied, and myriads more dragged into the bafeft flavery.

7. " But the furnifhing us with flaves is neceffary,
for the trade, and wealth, and glory of our nation:"
here are feveral miftakes. For 1. Wealth is not
neceffary to the glory of any nation; but wifdom, virtue, juftice, mercy, generofity, public fpirit, love of
our country. Thefe are neceffary to the real glory of
a nation; but abundance of wealth is not. Men of
underftanding allow, that the glory of *England* was
full as high, in Queen *Elizabeth's* time as it is now :
although our riches and trade were then as much
fmaller, as our virtue was greater. But, fecondly, it
is not clear, that we fhould have either lefs money or
trade, (only leis of that deteftable trade of man-fteal-
ing) if there was not a negro in all our Iflands, or in all
Englifh America. It is demonftrable, white men, inured
to it by degrees *can* work as well as them : and they
would do it, were negroes out of the way, and proper
encouragement given them. However, thirdly, I come
back to the fame point : better no trade, than trade
procured by villany. It is far better to have no wealth,
than to gain wealth at the expence of virtue. Better
is honeft poverty, than all the riches bought by
the tears, and fweat and blood of our fellow-crea-
tures.

8. " However this be, it is neceffary when we have
flaves,

flaves, to ufe them with feverity." What, to whip them for eveiy petty offence, till they are all in gore blood ? To take that opportunity, of rubbing pepper and falt into their raw flefh ? To drop burning fealing-wax upon their fkin ? To caftrate them ? To cut off half their foot with an axe ? To hang them on gib-bets, that they may die by inches, with heat, and hun-ger, and thirft ? To pin them down to the ground, and then burn them by degrees; from the feet, to the head ? To roaft them alive?—When did a Turk or a Heathen find it neceffary to ufe a fellow-creature thus ?

I pray, to what end is this ufage neceffary ? " Why, to prevent their running away : and to keep them con-ftantly to their labour, that they may not idle away their time. So miferably ftupid is this race of men, yea, fo ftubborn and fo wicked." Allowing them to be as ftupid as you fay, to whom is that ftupidity owing ? Without queftion it lies altogether at the door of their inhuman mafters : who give them no means, no opportunity of improving their underftand-ing : and indeed leave them no motive, either from hope or fear, to attempt any fuch thing. They were no way remarkable for ftupidity, while they remained in their own country : the inhabitants of *Africa* where they have equal motives and equal means of improve-ment, are not inferior to the inhabitants of *Europe* : to fome of them they are greatly fuperior. Impartially furvey in their own country, the natives of *Benin*, and the natives of *Lapland*. Compare, (fetting prejudice afide) the *Samoeids* and the *Angolans*. And on which fide does the advantage lie, in point of underftanding ? Certainly the *African* is in no refpect inferior to the *European*. Their ftupidity therefore in our plantations is not natural ; otherwife than it is the natural effect of their condition. Confequently it is not their fault, but *your's* : you muft anfwer for it, before God and man.

9. " But their ftupidity is not the only reafon of our treating them with feverity. For it is hard to fay, which is the greateft, this or their ftubbornnefs and wickednefs."——It may be fo : But do not thefe as well as the other, lie at *your* door ; are not ftubborn-nefs, cunning, pilfering; and divers other vices, the

natural,

natural, neceſſary fruits of ſlavery·? Is not this an ob-
ſervation which has been made, in every age and nation ?———And what means have you uſed to remove
this ſtubbornneſs? Have you tried what mildneſs and
gentleneſs would do? I knew one that did: that had
prudence and patience to make the experiment: Mr.
Hugh Bryan, who then lived on the borders of *South-
Carolina*. And what was the effect? Why, that all
his negroes (and he had no ſmall number of them)
loved and reverenced him as a father, and chearfully
obeyed him out of love. Yea, they were more afraid
of a frown from *him*, than of many blows from an over-
ſeer. And what pains have *you* taken, what method
have *you* uſed, to reclaim them from their wickedneſs?
Have you carefully taught them,

" That there is a God, a wiſe, powerful, merciful
being, the Creator and Governor of heaven and earth?
That he has appointed a day wherein he will judge the
world, will take an account of all our thoughts, words
and actions? That in that day he will reward every
child of man according to his works: that " then the
righteous ſhall inherit the kingdom prepared for them
from the foundation of the world: and the wicked
ſhall be caſt into everlaſting fire, prepared for the devil
and his angels." If you have not done this, if you
have taken no pains or thought about the matter, can
you wonder at their wickedneſs? What wonder, if
they ſhould cut your throat? And if they did, whom
could you thank for it but yourſelf? You firſt acted
the villain in making them ſlaves, (whether you ſtole
them or bought them.) You kept them ſtupid and
wicked, by cutting them off from all opportunities of
improving either in knowledge or virtue: and now
you aſſign their want of wiſdom and goodneſs as
the reaſon for uſing them worſe than brute beaſts!

V. 1. It remains only to make a little application
of the preceding obſervations.—But to whom ſhould
that application be made? That may bear a queſtion.
Should we addreſs ourſelves to the public at large?
What effect can this have? It may inflame the world
againſt the guilty, but is not likely to remove that guilt.
Should we appeal to the *Engliſh* nation in general?
This alſo is ſtriking wide; and is never likely to procure any redreſs for the ſore evil we complain of.—Is
little

little would it in all probability avail, to apply to the Parliament. So many things, which *seem* of greater importance lie before them that they are not likely to attend to this. I therefore add a few words to those who are more immediately concerned, whether captains, merchants or planters.

2. And, first, to the captains employed in this trade. Most of *you* know, the country of *Guinea*: several parts of it at least, between the river *Senegal* and the kingdom of *Angola.* Perhaps now, by *your* means, part of it is become a dreary uncultivated wildernefs, the inhabitants being all murdered or carried away, so that there are none left to till the ground. But you well know, how populous, how fruitful, how pleasant it was a few years ago. You know the people were not stupid, not wanting in fenfe, confidering the few means of improvement they enjoyed. Neither did you find them favage, fierce, cruel, treacherous, or unkind to strangers. On the contrary, they were in most parts, a fenfible and ingenious people. They were kind and friendly, courteous and obliging, and remarkably fair and just in their dealings. Such are the men whom you hire their own countrymen, to tear away from this lovely country ; part by stealth, part by force, part made captive in those wars, which you raife or foment on purpofe. You have feen them torn away, children from their parents, parents from their children : hufbands from their wives, wives from their beloved hufbands, brethren and fifters from each other. You have dragged them who had never done you any wrong, perhaps in chains, from their native fhore. You have forced them into your fhips like an herd of fwine, them who had fouls immortal as your own : (only fome of them, leaped into the fea, and refolutely stayed under water, till they could fuffer no more from you. You have stowed them together as clofe as ever they could lie, without any regard either to decency or convenience. And when many of them had been poifoned by foul air, or had funk under various hardfhips, you have feen their remains delivered to the deep, till the fea fhould give up its dead. You have carried the furvivors into the vileft flavery, never to end but with life: fuch flavery as is not found among the

the Turks. at *Algiers*, no nor among the Heathens in *America*.

3. May I fpeak plainly to you? I muft. Love con-
ftrains me : love to *you*, as well a to thofe you are concerned with.

Is there a God? You know there is. Is he a juft
God? Then there muft be a ftate of retribution : a
ftate wherein the juft God will reward every man according to his works. Then what reward will he render to *you*? O think betimes! Before you drop into
eternity! Think now, *He fhall have judgment without
mercy that hath fhewed no mercy.* Are you a *man*? Then
you fhould have a *human* heart. But have you indeed? What is your heart made of? Is there no fuch
principle as compaffion there? Do you never *feel*
another's pain? Have you no fympathy? No fenfe of
human woe? No pity for the miferable? When you
faw the flourifhing eyes, the heaving breafts, or the
bleeding fides and tortured limbs of your fellow-
creatures, was you a ftone, or a brute? Did you look
upon them with the eyes of a tiger? When you
fqueezed the agonizing creatures down in the fhip, or
when you threw their poor mangled remains into the
fea, had you no relenting? Did not one tear drop from
your eye, one figh efcape from your breaft? Do you
feel no relenting *now*? If you do not, you muft go on,
till the meafure of your iniquities is full. Then will
the great God deal with *you*, as you have dealt with
them, and require all their blood at your hands. And
at that day it fhall be more tolerable for Sodom and
Gomorrah than for *you*! But if your heart does relent,
though in a fmall degree, know it is a call from the
God of love. And to-day, if you will hear his voice,
harden not your heart. To-day refolve, God being
your helper, to efcape for your life. Regard not money!
All that a man hath will he give for his life! Whatever you lofe, lofe not your foul : nothing can counter-
vail that lofs. Immediately quit the horrid trade : at
all events, be an honeft man.

4. This equally concerns every Merchant, who is
engaged in the Slave-trade. It is *you* that induce the
African villain to fell his countrymen ; and in order
thereto, to fteal, rob, murder men, women and children without number: by enabling the *Englifh* villain

to

to pay him for fo doing; whom you over pay for his execrable labour. It is *your* money, that is the fpring of all, that impowers·him to go on : fo that whatever he or the *African* does in this matter, is all *your* act and deed. And is your confcience quite reconciled to this ?. Does it never reproach you at all ? Has gold entirely blinded your eyes, and ftupified your heart ? Can you fee, can you *feel* no harm therein ? Is it doing as you would be done to ? Make the cafe your own. " Mafter, faid a Slave at *Liverpool* (to the Merchant that owned him) "what if fome of my countrymen were to come here, and take away my miftrefs, and mafter *Tommy* and mafter *Billy* and carry them into our country, and make them flaves, how would you like it ?" His an-fwcr was worthy of a man : " I will never buy a flave more while I live." O let his refolution be your's! Have no more any part in this deteftable bufinefs. In-ftantly leave it to thofe unfeeling wretches, " Who laugh at human nature and compaffion ! Be *you* a man ! Not a wolf, a devourer of the human fpecies ! Be mer-ciful, that you may obtain mercy !

5. And this equally concerns every gentleman that has an cftate in our *American* plantations : yea all Slave-holders of whatever rank and degree : feeing *men-buyers* are exactly on a level with *men-ftealers*. Indeed you fay, " I pay honeftly for my goods : and I am not. concerned to know how they are come by : nay but you are : you are deeply concerned to know they are honeftly come by. Otherwife you are partaker with a thief, and are not a jot honefter than him. But you know, they are not honeftly come by : you know they are procured by means, nothing near fo innocent as picking pockets, houfe-breaking, or robbery upon the high-way. You know they are procured by a deliberate feries of more complicated villany, (of fraud. robbery and murder) than was ever practifed either by Mahome-tans or Pagans : in particular by murders of all kinds ; by the blood of the innocent poured upon the ground like water. Now it is *your* money that pays the Mer-chant, and through him the Captain, and the *African* butchers. *You* therefore are guilty, yea principally guilty, of all thefe frauds, robberies and murders. You are the fpring that puts all the reft in motion : they would not ftir a ftep without *you :* therefore the blood
of

of all thefe wretches, who die before their time, whether in the country or elfewhere, lies upon your head. *The blood of thy brother*, (for, whether thou wilt believe it or no, fuch he is in the fight of Him that made him) *crieth againft thee from the earth*, from the fhip, and from the waters. O, whatever it cofts, put a ftop to its cry before it be too late: inftantly, at any price, were it the half of your goods, deliver thyfelf from blood-guiltinefs! Thy hands, thy bed, thy furniture, thy houfe, thy lands are at prefent ftained with blood. Surely it is enough; accumulate no more guilt: fpill no more the blood of the innocent! Do not hire another to fhed blood: do not pay him for doing it! Whether you are a Chriftian or no, fhew yourfelf a man! Be not more favage than a lion or a bear!

6. Perhaps you will fay, "I do not *buy* any Negroes: I only *ufe* thofe left by my father." So far is well: but is it enough to fatisfy your own confcience? Had your father, have you, has any man living, a right to ufe another as a flave? It cannot be, even fetting revelation afide. It cannot be that either war, or contract, can give any man fuch a property in another as he has in his fheep and oxen. Much lefs is it poffible, that any child of man, fhould ever be *born a flave*. Liberty is the right of every human creature, as foon as he breathes the vital air. And no human law can deprive him of that right, which he derives from the law of nature.

If therefore you have any regard to juftice,-(to fay nothing of mercy, nor the revealed law of God) render unto all their due. Give liberty to whom liberty is due, that is to every child of man, to every partaker of human nature. Let none ferve you but by his own act and deed, by his own voluntary choice. Away with all whips, all chains, all compulfion! Be gentle toward all men, and fee that you invariably do unto every one, as you would he fhould do unto you.

7. O thou God of love, thou who art loving to every man, and whofe mercy is over all thy works; thou who art the Father of the fpirits of all flefh, and who art rich in mercy unto all; thou who has mingled of one blood all the nations upon the earth; have compaffion upon thefe out-cafts of men, who are trodden down as dung upon the earth! Arife and help thefe that have no helper, whofe-blood is fpilt upon the ground like water! Are not thefe alfo the work of thine own hands, the purchafe of thy Son's blood? Stir them up to cry unto thee, in the land of their captivity; and let their complaint come up before thee; let it enter into thy ears! Make even thofe that lead them away captive to pity them, and turn their captivity as the rivers in the South....O burft thou all their chains in funder; more efpecially the chains of their fins: Thou, Saviour of all, make them free, that they may be free indeed;

The fervile progeny of *Ham*
    Seize as the purchafe of thy blood!
Let all the Heathens know thy name,
    From Idols to the living God;
The dark *Americans* convert,
    And fhine in every Pagan heart.

F I N I S.